YORK NOTES

# THE STRANGE CASE OF DR JEKYLL AND MR HYDE

## AQA PRACTICE TESTS WITH ANSWERS

**ANNE ROONEY**

Pearson

YORK PRESS

The right of Anne Rooney to be identified as the Author of this Work
has been asserted by her in accordance with the Copyright,
Designs and Patents Act 1988

YORK PRESS
322 Old Brompton Road, London SW5 9JH

PEARSON EDUCATION LIMITED
Edinburgh Gate, Harlow,
Essex CM20 2JE, United Kingdom
Associated companies, branches and representatives throughout the world

First published 2018

10 9 8 7 6 5 4 3 2 1

ISBN 978–1–2922–3684–1

Phototypeset by Swales and Willis Ltd
Printed in Slovakia

*Photo credits*: Elnur/Shutterstock for page 6 bottom / Monkey Business Images/
Shutterstock for page 50 bottom

# CONTENTS

# PART ONE: INTRODUCTION

## How to use these practice tests

This book contains seven GCSE English Literature exam-style practice tests for *The Strange Case of Dr Jekyll and Mr Hyde*. All the York Notes tests have been modelled on the ones that you will sit in your AQA GCSE 9–1 English Literature exam.

There are lots of ways these tests can support your study and revision for your AQA English Literature exam on *The Strange Case of Dr Jekyll and Mr Hyde*. There is no 'right' way – choose the one (or ones) that suits your learning style best.

### 1  Alongside the York Notes Study Guide for *The Strange Case of Dr Jekyll and Mr Hyde*

Do you have the York Notes Study Guide for *The Strange Case of Dr Jekyll and Mr Hyde*?

These tests will allow you to try out all the skills and techniques outlined in the Study Guide. So you could:

- choose a question from this book
- read the sections of the Study Guide relevant to the question, i.e. Plot and Action; Characters; Themes, Contexts and Setting; Structure, Form and Language
- use the Progress Booster exam section of the Study Guide to remind yourself of key exam techniques
- complete the question.

### 2  As a stand-alone revision programme

Do you know the text inside out and have you already mastered the skills needed for your exam?

If so, you can keep your skills fresh by answering one or two questions from this book each day or week in the lead-up to the exam. You could make a revision diary and allocate particular questions to particular times.

### 3  As a form of mock exam

Would you like to test yourself under exam conditions?

You could put aside part of a day to work on a practice test in a quiet room. Set a stopwatch so that you can experience what it will be like in your real exam. If some of your friends have copies of this book then several of you could all do this together and discuss your answers afterwards.

Or, you could try working through Part Two of this book slowly, question by question, over a number of days as part of your revision, and save the further questions in Part Three to use as a mock test nearer the exam.

## How to use the answer sections

This book contains a mixture of annotated sample answers and short (indicative content) answers that will help you to:

- identify the difference between Mid, Good and Very High Level work
- understand how the Assessment Objectives are applied
- grade your own answers by comparing them with the samples provided.

The answers can also give you additional ideas for your responses and help you to aim high.

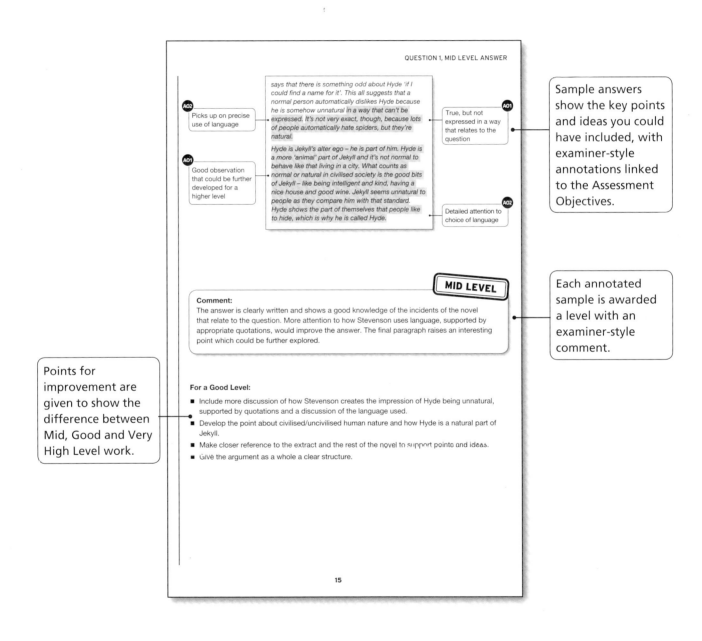

QUESTION 1, MID LEVEL ANSWER

**AO2** Picks up on precise use of language

*says that there is something odd about Hyde 'if I could find a name for it'. This all suggests that a normal person automatically dislikes Hyde because he is somehow unnatural in a way that can't be expressed. It's not very exact, though, because lots of people automatically hate spiders, but they're natural.*

**AO1** True, but not expressed in a way that relates to the question

**AO1** Good observation that could be further developed for a higher level

*Hyde is Jekyll's alter ego – he is part of him. Hyde is a more 'animal' part of Jekyll and it's not normal to behave like that living in a city. What counts as normal or natural in civilised society is the good bits of Jekyll – like being intelligent and kind, having a nice house and good wine. Jekyll seems unnatural to people as they compare him with that standard. Hyde shows the part of themselves that people like to hide, which is why he is called Hyde.*

**AO2** Detailed attention to choice of language

**MID LEVEL**

**Comment:**
The answer is clearly written and shows a good knowledge of the incidents of the novel that relate to the question. More attention to how Stevenson uses language, supported by appropriate quotations, would improve the answer. The final paragraph raises an interesting point which could be further explored.

**For a Good Level:**
- Include more discussion of how Stevenson creates the impression of Hyde being unnatural, supported by quotations and a discussion of the language used.
- Develop the point about civilised/uncivilised human nature and how Hyde is a natural part of Jekyll.
- Make closer reference to the extract and the rest of the novel to support points and ideas.
- Give the argument as a whole a clear structure.

15

Sample answers show the key points and ideas you could have included, with examiner-style annotations linked to the Assessment Objectives.

Each annotated sample is awarded a level with an examiner-style comment.

Points for improvement are given to show the difference between Mid, Good and Very High Level work.

## Assessment Objectives and weightings

Your work on *The Strange Case of Dr Jekyll and Mr Hyde* will be examined through the three Assessment Objectives (AOs) listed below:

| AO1 | Read, understand and respond to texts. You should be able to:<br>● maintain a critical style and develop an informed personal response<br>● use textual references, including quotations, to support and illustrate interpretations. |
|---|---|
| AO2 | Analyse the language, form and structure used by a writer to create meanings and effects, using relevant subject terminology where appropriate. |
| AO3 | Show understanding of the relationships between texts and the contexts in which they were written. |

The marks allocated by AQA for each Assessment Objective are as follows:

| AO1 | 12 marks |
|---|---|
| AO2 | 12 marks |
| AO3 | 6 marks |
| **Total (per question)** | 30 marks |

Knowing the number of marks allowed for each AO is important, as this will help you to achieve the right balance of key skills and techniques in your answer.

## Mark scheme

The annotated sample answers that follow Questions 1 to 4 in this book have been given a Level based on the mark schemes below.*

### Lower Level

| AO1 | You give some relevant responses to the set task and use some suitable references. |
|-----|-----------------------------------------------------------------------------------|
| AO2 | You identify some of the writer's methods but do not always comment effectively on them. |
| AO3 | You show some awareness of contextual factors but find it difficult to link them to the text. |

### Mid Level

| AO1 | You give a clear response and select suitable references and quotations. |
|-----|-------------------------------------------------------------------------|
| AO2 | You make clear references to the writer's methods to support your points. |
| AO3 | You make clear links between some aspects of context and the text. |

Turn to page 8 for the mark schemes for Good to High and Very High Levels.

* These are 'student-friendly' mark schemes and are a guide only.

**Good to High Level**

| AO1 | You demonstrate very effective understanding of the task and text, and choose references and quotations carefully. |
| --- | --- |
| AO2 | You analyse carefully and comment consistently well on the writer's methods, interpreting ideas. |
| AO3 | You make very effective links between context and the text. |

**Very High Level**

| AO1 | You have a broad, conceptualised idea of the text, and make well-judged and wide-ranging use of references and quotations. |
| --- | --- |
| AO2 | You are analytical and explore the text precisely and convincingly. You comment in finely tuned detail on the writer's use of language, form and structure. |
| AO3 | You write convincingly and relevantly about a wide range of contextual factors. |

Now you know what you're aiming for, you can begin the practice tests.

Turn to page 10 for Question 1.*

* *The extracts from* The Strange Case of Dr Jekyll and Mr Hyde *used in these Practice Tests are taken from the Penguin English Library edition, 2012.*

# PART TWO: YORK NOTES PRACTICE TESTS WITH ANNOTATED SAMPLE ANSWERS

## Question 1

Read the following extract from *The Strange Case of Dr Jekyll and Mr Hyde* (Chapter Nine, page 53).

In this extract, Dr Lanyon describes his first impressions of Mr Hyde.

> Here, at last, I had a chance of clearly seeing him. I had never set eyes on him before, so much was certain. He was small, as I have said; I was struck besides with the shocking expression of his face, with his remarkable combination of great muscular
> 5 activity and great apparent debility of constitution, and – last but not least – with the odd, subjective disturbance caused by his neighbourhood. This bore some resemblance to incipient rigor, and was accompanied by a marked sinking of the pulse. At the time, I set it down to some idiosyncratic, personal distaste, and merely
> 10 wondered at the acuteness of the symptoms; but I have since had reason to believe the cause to lie much deeper in the nature of man, and to turn on some nobler hinge than the principle of hatred.
>
> This person (who had thus, from the first moment of his entrance, struck in me what I can only describe as a disgustful curiosity)
> 15 was dressed in a fashion that would have made an ordinary person laughable: his clothes, that is to say, although they were of rich and sober fabric, were enormously too large for him in every measurement – the trousers hanging on his legs and rolled up to keep them from the ground, the waist of the coat below
> 20 his haunches, and the collar sprawling wide upon his shoulders. Strange to relate, this ludicrous accoutrement was far from moving me to laughter. Rather, as there was something abnormal and misbegotten in the very essence of the creature that now faced me – something seizing, surprising and revolting – this fresh disparity
> 25 seemed but to fit in with and to reinforce it; so that to my interest in the man's nature and character, there was added a curiosity as to his origin, his life, his fortune and status in the world.

Starting with this extract, explore how Stevenson presents Mr Hyde's unnaturalness.

Write about:

- how Stevenson presents Hyde's unnaturalness through Dr Lanyon's description
- how Stevenson presents Hyde's unnaturalness throughout the novel.

**[30 marks]**

## Annotated sample answers

Now, read the three sample answers that follow and, based on what you have read, try to allocate a level to your own work. Which of the three responses is your answer closest to? Don't be discouraged if your work doesn't seem as strong as some of the responses here – the point is to use these samples to learn about what is needed and then put it into practice in your own work. Conversely, you may have mentioned relevant ideas or points which don't appear in these responses; if this is the case, give yourself a pat on the back – it shows you are considering lots of good ideas!

### Sample answer A

**AO1** Starts with clear topic sentence relating to question

*Hyde is shown as unnatural throughout the novel. Here, it's Dr Lanyon who finds him unnatural. He has just let Hyde into his room to collect the potion. He immediately dislikes Hyde; we learn just before the extract that he keeps his hand on his gun because he doesn't trust him. Lanyon describes the ways Hyde is odd: he wears clothes that are too big, he has a 'shocking expression' on his face and 'incipient rigor' and a slow pulse. Dr Lanyon thinks he is just being silly and it's only 'personal distaste' that makes him dislike Hyde. But later he decided there was something else. He doesn't say what, though – just that there is something 'deeper in the nature of man' that turned him against Hyde. This is vague and not very helpful, but perhaps that's because he doesn't understand it himself.*

**AO1** These are symptoms Lanyon finds in himself, they are not features of Hyde

**AO1** A reasonable comment

*Hyde is unnatural every time he turns up in the story. The first time is when he tramples a small child. A normal person would stop and make sure the child was all right, but Hyde doesn't. This shows he is not a normal person. The other people there hate him, because he has done a bad thing and isn't sorry. Later, his attack on Sir Danvers Carew for no reason is a worse example of the same thing. We might think he is a psychopath, but in the 19th century they didn't have proper terms for different sorts of mental illness. But there would still have been people with mental problems, so Stevenson and his readers might have met people who behaved like this. If he is mad, he still seems unnatural. The rest of the novel shows he is unnatural in a more scary way, though.*

**AO3** Attempt to relate to historical context, but poorly expressed

*No one likes Hyde, except maybe Jekyll who finds him thrilling as well as frightening. Everyone else feels uneasy around him, and finds him revolting. Utterson says he is 'hardly human', and gives him a feeling of 'disgust, loathing and fear'. Hyde is linked with the devil several times. No one can explain what about Hyde is so hideous. Enfield, Lanyon and Utterson all try to pin it down, but they can't. Enfield says the look of Hyde made him sweat, and Utterson*

**AO2** Appropriate quotations properly embedded

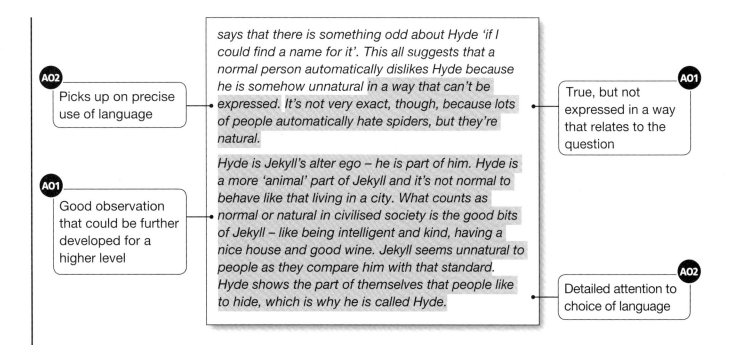

**AO2** — Picks up on precise use of language

**AO1** — Good observation that could be further developed for a higher level

*says that there is something odd about Hyde 'if I could find a name for it'. This all suggests that a normal person automatically dislikes Hyde because he is somehow unnatural in a way that can't be expressed. It's not very exact, though, because lots of people automatically hate spiders, but they're natural.*

*Hyde is Jekyll's alter ego – he is part of him. Hyde is a more 'animal' part of Jekyll and it's not normal to behave like that living in a city. What counts as normal or natural in civilised society is the good bits of Jekyll – like being intelligent and kind, having a nice house and good wine. Jekyll seems unnatural to people as they compare him with that standard. Hyde shows the part of themselves that people like to hide, which is why he is called Hyde.*

**AO1** — True, but not expressed in a way that relates to the question

**AO2** — Detailed attention to choice of language

**MID LEVEL**

**Comment:**
The answer is clearly written and shows a good knowledge of the incidents of the novel that relate to the question. More attention to how Stevenson uses language, supported by appropriate quotations, would improve the answer. The final paragraph raises an interesting point which could be further explored.

**For a Good Level:**

- Include more discussion of how Stevenson creates the impression of Hyde being unnatural, supported by quotations and a discussion of the language used.
- Develop the point about civilised/uncivilised human nature and how Hyde is a natural part of Jekyll.
- Make closer reference to the extract and the rest of the novel to support points and ideas.
- Give the argument as a whole a clear structure.

## Sample answer B

**AO1**
Clear placing of the extract in its context in the novel

*This passage is in the letter that Dr Lanyon leaves for Utterson explaining why he has fallen out with Jekyll and describing what he has seen. Lanyon does not believe in the supernatural. He has argued before with Jekyll about Jekyll's unscientific 'fanciful' notions. Because of his views, Lanyon tries to explain why he is revolted by Hyde by giving factual details about how he looks. In other words he talks about what Hyde is wearing, the 'shocking expression' on his face, and his 'debility of constitution', which means he's not in a good way. But this doesn't really account for how Lanyon feels, and he ends up saying there is something 'abnormal and misbegotten' in Hyde that he can't explain. By using the word 'misbegotten', Stevenson suggests that Hyde is not the product of normal human reproduction and birth, which would certainly make him unnatural. Because we know Lanyon doesn't usually trust supernatural explanations, this view carries weight.*

**AO1**
Draws on other areas of the novel to support the account of Lanyon's viewpoint

**AO2**
Appropriate choice of quotation, properly embedded

**AO2**
Careful analysis of word choice and its effects

*Other characters also decide that Hyde is unnatural. Mr Utterson first hears about Hyde from Mr Enfield, who tells him about an unnatural act: Hyde running down and trampling on a small child. Enfield says that he and the people who saw it happen reacted with instant hatred towards Hyde. He described Hyde as a 'damnable man' – linking Hyde with the devil. Enfield says the doctor was 'turning white and sick with desire to kill him' – a similar reaction to Lanyon later. Utterson waits for Hyde for ages and when he finally sees him, he is disgusted by him and feels 'loathing and fear' at a man who 'seems hardly human'. He says he thinks Hyde has a 'foul soul' that is something normal people can pick up on.*

**AO1**
Establishes the first hint of unnaturalness

**AO2**
Apt quotations, well embedded, but more comment on their effect is needed

*Whenever Hyde is described, he seems repulsive. When Utterson and Poole find his dead body, it is horrifying, 'sorely contorted and still twitching'. And when Jekyll describes looking down to see Hyde's hand when he first changes without using his potion, it sounds unpleasant: 'lean, corded, knuckly', a nasty pale colour and covered with black hair. The most important sign that Hyde is unnatural, though, is the way other people respond to him. He always produces a sense of horror, repulsion or fear. The better-educated characters, Lanyon and Utterson, try to find good reasons for their responses but they can't. These are professional people who try to use their learning to explain things, while the uneducated characters are less sophisticated. Stevenson reflects Victorian ideas about the educated and uneducated classes in this. Lanyon and Utterson can't explain*

**AO2**
This might be ugly, but is not by itself unnatural

**AO2**
True, but make it clear Stevenson has chosen to convey his unnaturalness in this way

**AO1**
Correct assessment but could be explored further with clear textual reference

**AO3**
Reference to contemporary attitudes to class and learning

*their response to Hyde and are left feeling something inside them rejects him instinctively.*

*One other reason Hyde seems unnatural is because Stevenson presents him as pure evil. He is all the bad aspects of Jekyll with none of the good parts. It is unnatural for the parts of someone's personality to be split like this, even though it is natural for an individual to include both good and bad aspects. This would mean that although Hyde is unnatural on his own, as part of Jekyll he would be natural. The unnaturalness is in being pulled out of Jekyll to go around on its own.*

**AO1**
Working towards a sophisticated understanding, but dealt with rather superficially

*Overall, Stevenson uses descriptions of Hyde, the responses of other characters, and Hyde's behaviour – like trampling a child and not being sorry, or beating an old man to death – to show he is thoroughly unnatural.*

**AO1**
Fair attempt at summing up, which relates back to the question

**GOOD LEVEL**

**Comment:**
A good answer that shows a sound grasp of the novel and examines the extract briefly. A more careful investigation of how Stevenson uses language to create effects, both in the extract and elsewhere, would make this a better answer. Quotations are well selected and used effectively. There are some well-expressed ideas, but better organisation and a clearer structure would give them stronger impact on the reader.

**For a High Level:**

■ Include more detailed analysis of how Stevenson's choices of words, phraseology, syntax and structure help to create effects.

■ Pay more attention to the structure and argument of the answer.

■ Make more detailed reference to the social, literary and historical context of the novel.

## Sample answer C

**AO1** Introduction sets out the line of argument the answer will take

Stevenson presents Hyde as unnatural throughout the novel and through the eyes of several characters, but we might question how far this conclusion is finally borne out by the tale.

In this extract, Lanyon, a doctor, tries to view Hyde professionally, but even he is entirely repulsed by him, underlining the unnaturalness of Hyde. Lanyon finds something 'abnormal and misbegotten' in the 'creature' in front of him. The word 'creature' denies Hyde's humanity. Lanyon tries to pin down what is odd about Hyde by describing it in scientific language: he refers to 'great muscular activity' and 'debility of constitution', meaning that he seems weak and perhaps ill.

**AO1** Very well-chosen quotations, skilfully embedded

**AO2** Detailed analysis of language and its effects

Lanyon is surprised by his own response – an 'incipient rigor', and a 'marked sinking of the pulse', describing his symptoms as he would describe them in a patient. He wonders if he just has an 'idiosyncratic' personal dislike of Hyde but as he thinks about it he suspects something 'nobler' causes him to recoil from Hyde. This is particularly powerful because we know Lanyon is scornful of anything that seems supernatural, so he must feel it very strongly in order to say this.

**AO2** Continued analysis of choice of language

**AO1** Relation to what we learn of a character elsewhere in the novel

Dr Lanyon is not the only character who reacts to Hyde with disgust. Stevenson introduces Hyde through Mr Enfield's account of him trampling a child. Enfield's response is also one of revulsion; he reports 'loathing' Hyde at 'first sight', noticing even the doctor 'turning white and sick with desire to kill him'. Indeed, the entire crowd is hostile, the women 'wild as harpies' – it seems that Hyde brings out the unnatural or inhuman in others, too, as harpies are half-bird, half-human figures from Greek myth.

**AO1** Links the extract to the rest of the novel

**AO1** Very apt quotations successfully embedded

**AO3** Explanation of reference and assessment of how it's used

When Mr Utterson finally encounters Hyde, he tries to explain the source of the 'disgust, loathing and fear' he feels. Hyde 'seems hardly human', and there is something 'troglodytic' about him. 'Troglodytic' means someone who lives underground or in a cave, which is not a normal human way to live and suggests Hyde is troll-like or primitive. Utterson thinks of a popular rhyme which starts: 'I do not like thee Dr Fell, The reason why I cannot tell.' This suggests an unidentifiable, mysterious source for his dislike that recalls something mythic and archetypal. He suggests that Hyde has a 'foul soul' that somehow manifests itself in his body. This ties in with the common belief at the time that physical appearance, and in particular facial features, were a clue to personality.

**AO2** Shows detailed understanding of the term and the effect it creates

**AO3** Relevant contextual reference and explanation

**AO3** Good link to contemporary theories of physiognomy

Even minor characters are disgusted by Hyde. The maid recognises Hyde as someone she had already 'conceived a dislike' for, and his landlady is pleased to learn he is in trouble. Even Poole, who has to be polite,

**AO1** Clear signalling of essay's structure

**AO1** Detailed reference to other parts of the novel, showing a thorough knowledge of the text

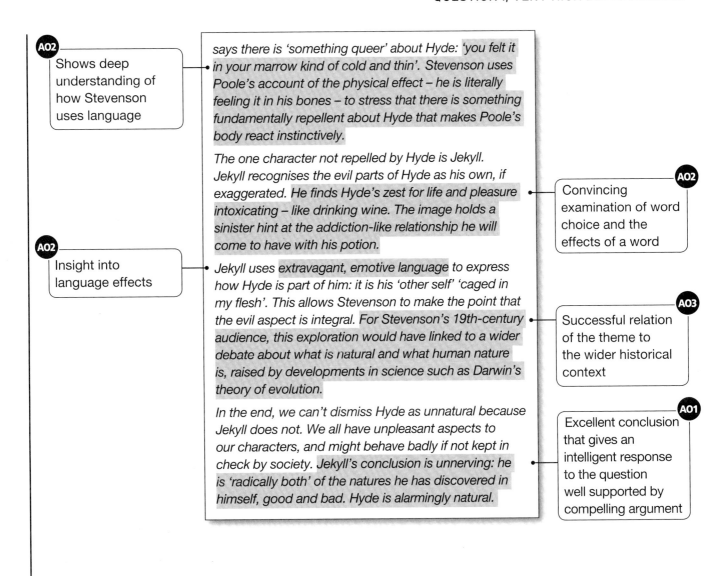

**AO2**
Shows deep understanding of how Stevenson uses language

**AO2**
Insight into language effects

says there is 'something queer' about Hyde: 'you felt it in your marrow kind of cold and thin'. Stevenson uses Poole's account of the physical effect – he is literally feeling it in his bones – to stress that there is something fundamentally repellent about Hyde that makes Poole's body react instinctively.

The one character not repelled by Hyde is Jekyll. Jekyll recognises the evil parts of Hyde as his own, if exaggerated. He finds Hyde's zest for life and pleasure intoxicating – like drinking wine. The image holds a sinister hint at the addiction-like relationship he will come to have with his potion.

Jekyll uses extravagant, emotive language to express how Hyde is part of him: it is his 'other self' 'caged in my flesh'. This allows Stevenson to make the point that the evil aspect is integral. For Stevenson's 19th-century audience, this exploration would have linked to a wider debate about what is natural and what human nature is, raised by developments in science such as Darwin's theory of evolution.

In the end, we can't dismiss Hyde as unnatural because Jekyll does not. We all have unpleasant aspects to our characters, and might behave badly if not kept in check by society. Jekyll's conclusion is unnerving: he is 'radically both' of the natures he has discovered in himself, good and bad. Hyde is alarmingly natural.

**AO2**
Convincing examination of word choice and the effects of a word

**AO3**
Successful relation of the theme to the wider historical context

**AO1**
Excellent conclusion that gives an intelligent response to the question well supported by compelling argument

**VERY HIGH LEVEL**

**Comment:**
A thorough and well-organised answer that presents very high-level ideas in an intelligent exploration of the question and shows an excellent grasp of the novel as a whole. The answer remains focused on the question, and successfully challenges the terms of the question in finding Hyde natural in the end. There is appropriate reference to the social and historical context of the novel and detailed analysis of Stevenson's choice of language and its effects.

## Question 2

Read the following extract from *The Strange Case of Dr Jekyll and Mr Hyde* (Chapter Eight, pages 40–1).

In this extract, Poole is trying to persuade Mr Utterson that Dr Jekyll has been murdered.

'That's it!' said Poole. 'It was this way. I came suddenly into the theatre from the garden. It seems he had slipped out to look for this drug or whatever it is; for the cabinet door was open, and there he was at the far end of the room digging among the crates.
5    He looked up when I came in, gave a kind of cry, and whipped upstairs into the cabinet. It was but for one minute that I saw him, but the hair stood upon my head like quills. Sir, if that was my master, why had he a mask upon his face? If it was my master, why did he cry out like a rat, and run from me? I have served him
10   long enough. And then ...' The man paused and passed his hand over his face.

'These are all very strange circumstances,' said Mr Utterson, 'but I think I begin to see daylight. Your master, Poole, is plainly seized with one of those maladies that both torture and deform the
15   sufferer; hence, for aught I know, the alteration of his voice; hence the mask and the avoidance of his friends; hence his eagerness to find this drug, by means of which the poor soul retains some hope of ultimate recovery – God grant that he be not deceived! There is my explanation; it is sad enough, Poole, ay, and appalling
20   to consider; but it is plain and natural, hangs well together and delivers us from all exorbitant alarms.'

Starting with this extract, explore how Stevenson presents the story from different perspectives.

Write about:

- how Stevenson uses the perspectives of Poole and Utterson in the extract
- how Stevenson uses other perspectives to present the story.

**[30 marks]**

## Annotated sample answers

Now, read the three sample answers that follow and, based on what you have read, try to allocate a level to your own work. Which of the three responses is your answer closest to? Don't be discouraged if your work doesn't seem as strong as some of the responses here – the point is to use these samples to learn about what is needed and then put it into practice in your own work. Conversely, you may have mentioned relevant ideas or points which don't appear in these responses; if this is the case, give yourself a pat on the back – it shows you are considering lots of good ideas!

### Sample answer A

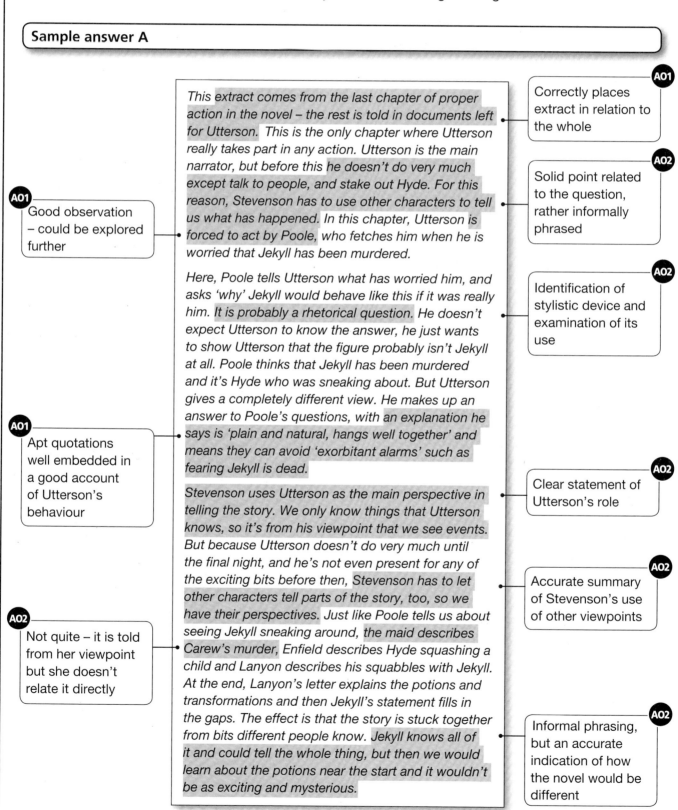

**AO1** Good observation – could be explored further

**AO1** Apt quotations well embedded in a good account of Utterson's behaviour

**AO2** Not quite – it is told from her viewpoint but she doesn't relate it directly

*This extract comes from the last chapter of proper action in the novel – the rest is told in documents left for Utterson. This is the only chapter where Utterson really takes part in any action. Utterson is the main narrator, but before this he doesn't do very much except talk to people, and stake out Hyde. For this reason, Stevenson has to use other characters to tell us what has happened. In this chapter, Utterson is forced to act by Poole, who fetches him when he is worried that Jekyll has been murdered.*

*Here, Poole tells Utterson what has worried him, and asks 'why' Jekyll would behave like this if it was really him. It is probably a rhetorical question. He doesn't expect Utterson to know the answer, he just wants to show Utterson that the figure probably isn't Jekyll at all. Poole thinks that Jekyll has been murdered and it's Hyde who was sneaking about. But Utterson gives a completely different view. He makes up an answer to Poole's questions, with an explanation he says is 'plain and natural, hangs well together' and means they can avoid 'exorbitant alarms' such as fearing Jekyll is dead.*

*Stevenson uses Utterson as the main perspective in telling the story. We only know things that Utterson knows, so it's from his viewpoint that we see events. But because Utterson doesn't do very much until the final night, and he's not even present for any of the exciting bits before then, Stevenson has to let other characters tell parts of the story, too, so we have their perspectives. Just like Poole tells us about seeing Jekyll sneaking around, the maid describes Carew's murder, Enfield describes Hyde squashing a child and Lanyon describes his squabbles with Jekyll. At the end, Lanyon's letter explains the potions and transformations and then Jekyll's statement fills in the gaps. The effect is that the story is stuck together from bits different people know. Jekyll knows all of it and could tell the whole thing, but then we would learn about the potions near the start and it wouldn't be as exciting and mysterious.*

**AO1** Correctly places extract in relation to the whole

**AO2** Solid point related to the question, rather informally phrased

**AO2** Identification of stylistic device and examination of its use

**AO2** Clear statement of Utterson's role

**AO2** Accurate summary of Stevenson's use of other viewpoints

**AO2** Informal phrasing, but an accurate indication of how the novel would be different

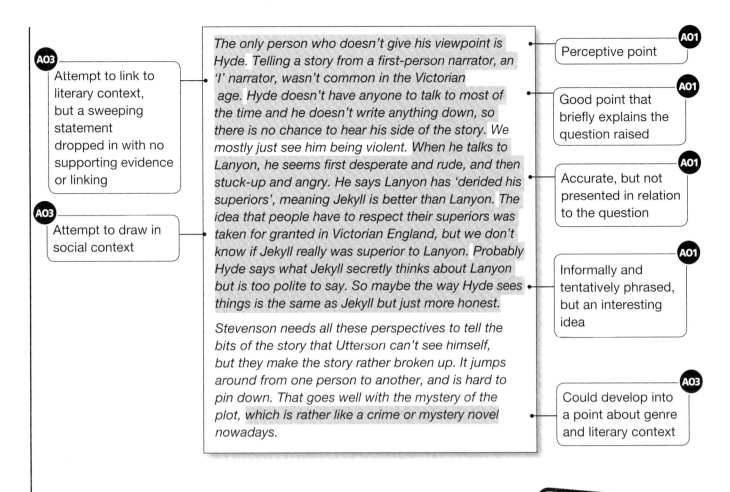

**AO3** Attempt to link to literary context, but a sweeping statement dropped in with no supporting evidence or linking

**AO3** Attempt to draw in social context

> *The only person who doesn't give his viewpoint is Hyde. Telling a story from a first-person narrator, an 'I' narrator, wasn't common in the Victorian age. Hyde doesn't have anyone to talk to most of the time and he doesn't write anything down, so there is no chance to hear his side of the story. We mostly just see him being violent. When he talks to Lanyon, he seems first desperate and rude, and then stuck-up and angry. He says Lanyon has 'derided his superiors', meaning Jekyll is better than Lanyon. The idea that people have to respect their superiors was taken for granted in Victorian England, but we don't know if Jekyll really was superior to Lanyon. Probably Hyde says what Jekyll secretly thinks about Lanyon but is too polite to say. So maybe the way Hyde sees things is the same as Jekyll but just more honest.*
>
> *Stevenson needs all these perspectives to tell the bits of the story that Utterson can't see himself, but they make the story rather broken up. It jumps around from one person to another, and is hard to pin down. That goes well with the mystery of the plot, which is rather like a crime or mystery novel nowadays.*

**AO1** Perceptive point

**AO1** Good point that briefly explains the question raised

**AO1** Accurate, but not presented in relation to the question

**AO1** Informally and tentatively phrased, but an interesting idea

**AO3** Could develop into a point about genre and literary context

## MID LEVEL

**Comment:**

A mid level answer that addresses the question in both the extract and the rest of the novel and shows a good understanding of the structure of the whole text. The phrasing is often informal and imprecise, sometimes seeming not to have been well-enough thought through and consolidated, but the points made are generally valid.

**For a Good Level:**

- Develop points into clear, well written statements supported with evidence from the text.
- Relate the novel to its social, historical and literary context in ways that are relevant to the question.
- Examine the use of language and the effects Stevenson achieves with it.
- Structure the answer as a clear argument or explanation, with points following one another logically and making clear links between them.

**Sample answer B**

**AO2** Identifies effects of Stevenson's use of direct speech

Stevenson uses the perspectives of many characters to put together the story in 'Dr Jekyll and Mr Hyde'. This extract gives the perspectives of two characters: Jekyll's butler, Poole, and his lawyer, Mr Utterson. The extract is all direct speech and there is not much direct speech in the novel. It therefore gives the characters' viewpoints directly.

**AO1** Good opening with a statement setting out to answer the question and relating directly to the extract

Poole is a minor character, but he knows Jekyll well and has seen Hyde coming and going. He tells Utterson exactly what he has seen – 'It was this way' – and suggests through his repeated question 'why' that Jekyll would not behave like this. He has already decided what he thinks: that Jekyll has been murdered. Utterson has a different idea: that Jekyll has an illness that makes him look deformed and so is hiding. The two characters make up their minds differently, following their different ways of looking at the situation. Utterson seems keen to make his idea sound convincing – 'it is plain and natural, hangs well together' – which suggests he is trying to persuade himself as well as Poole. Poole has a physical response to seeing someone scurrying about: 'the hair stood upon my head like quills'. Hyde often makes people immediately disgusted, so Poole's physical response supports his view that it's Hyde lurking between the crates. Utterson rejects the idea at first, but soon suggests 'we both think more than we have said', and forces Poole to 'make a clean breast of' his suspicion – to tell him what he's thinking.

**AO2** Clear interpretation of well-embedded quotation

**AO1** Clear distinction of different views of the same circumstance

**AO1** Fair analysis – needs relating more closely to the question

Because Stevenson has chosen to tell the story from Utterson's perspective, he needs a way of including events that Utterson doesn't see. He does this by making other characters describe what they have seen (Enfield and Poole), or leave a written document (Jekyll and Lanyon), or even telling part of the story as though narrated by another character (e.g. the maid). Although we are not given her words as direct speech, Carew's murder is told from her perspective using words that reflect hers. For instance, Hyde was 'carrying on (as the maid described it) like a madman'.

**AO1** Fair analysis

**AO2** Shows effect of Stevenson's choice of words

Extra characters don't only fill in details Utterson hasn't seen, they tell events in a way that ties in with what their personalities are like. So when Lanyon, a doctor, describes Hyde, he looks for physical details. When the landlady (chosen as 'unscrupulous') discovers Hyde is in trouble it is with 'a flash of odious joy' on her face. These different perspectives don't always agree. Stevenson seems to suggest we can't tell which account of something is actually true, as everyone tells it differently.

**AO1** Good link to the next point

**AO1** Interesting point that could be developed further

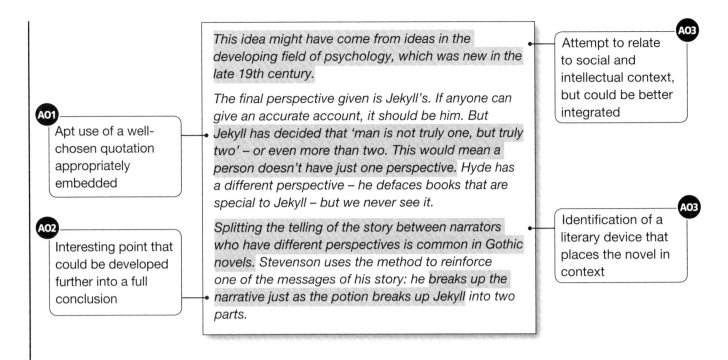

**AO3** Attempt to relate to social and intellectual context, but could be better integrated

**AO1** Apt use of a well-chosen quotation appropriately embedded

This idea might have come from ideas in the developing field of psychology, which was new in the late 19th century.

The final perspective given is Jekyll's. If anyone can give an accurate account, it should be him. But Jekyll has decided that 'man is not truly one, but truly two' – or even more than two. This would mean a person doesn't have just one perspective. Hyde has a different perspective – he defaces books that are special to Jekyll – but we never see it.

**AO3** Identification of a literary device that places the novel in context

**AO2** Interesting point that could be developed further into a full conclusion

Splitting the telling of the story between narrators who have different perspectives is common in Gothic novels. Stevenson uses the method to reinforce one of the messages of his story: he breaks up the narrative just as the potion breaks up Jekyll into two parts.

**GOOD LEVEL**

**Comment:**
An answer written at a consistently good level with some interesting and original ideas. There are some good points that are rather rushed over, that could be made more of – particularly the difficulty of interpreting events correctly or objectively, and the fragmenting of perspective within an individual. The answer has a clear structure and mostly addresses the question throughout.

**For a High Level:**

- Further develop the points of the difficulty of objectivity and of fractured personality, giving evidence from the text.

- Make more reference to the novel's context and integrate understanding of context into the answer.

- Give more detailed analysis of Stevenson's use of language in creating effects and making points.

## Sample answer C

**AO1**
Good opening relating the extract to the whole novel in the context of the question

*The structure of 'Dr Jekyll and Mr Hyde' relies on drawing together the perspectives of several characters who witness different parts of the story. In this extract, we see two perspectives.*

**AO2**
Careful and focused interpretation of language in detail

*The extract falls into two halves. First Poole relates an incident, then Utterson interprets it. Poole describes just what he saw – 'It was this way' – and, far from offering an explanation, he raises questions about it ('why … why …'). Utterson, on the other hand, invents a fanciful story to explain the scene. Although Utterson has no evidence for his view, his language suggests certainty. Saying Jekyll is 'plainly seized' by some illness makes it look as if this is clearly correct, and shuts down discussion. Utterson is trying to convince himself as well as Poole, and defends his version vigorously as 'plain and natural'. His lawyer's logic has failed him: an explanation is not automatically correct just because it 'hangs together well'.*

**AO2**
Good analysis of choice of language and its effects

**AO1**
Apt quotation skilfully embedded

*Utterson is our guide through the novel; we are tied to his perspective, but he sees very little first hand. To provide information that would not otherwise be available to Utterson – and so to us – Stevenson has other characters tell parts of the story, either directly or in written documents. Lanyon and eventually Jekyll make the most important contributions, but other characters play a vital role, too.*

**AO1**
Succinct summary of narratorial strategy and structure, introducing the next part of the answer

*Lanyon's perspective is given in his conversations with Utterson and in the letter he leaves for him. The conversations introduce the theme of science and prepare us for Jekyll's involvement with some kind of spiritual or metaphysical explorations. The letter contains the stunning revelation of Jekyll's transformation. Stevenson has chosen the most down-to-earth and scientifically reliable character as witness to this. What Lanyon sees is so at odds with his practical, scientific view of the world that his 'life is shaken to its roots'; the shock kills him. This extreme result stresses the reliability of his report.*

**AO1**
Apt quotation well used as evidence to support the point

*Where incidents are not witnessed by a main character, Stevenson has minor characters describe them. This begins with Enfield describing Hyde trampling a small child, continues with the account of Carew's murder told from the point of view of the maid who saw it, and even Hyde's landlady reporting on his movements. As well as his part in the chapter the extract is in, Poole tells Utterson that Hyde is free to come and go, but never dines at Jekyll's house.*

**AO1**
Sound structure for paragraph, making a point, supporting it with examples and evidence

*Utterson becomes more than a narrator; he is a curator of the story as he collects and interprets*

28

**AO3** Appropriate reference to wider literary context

**AO3** Good and relevant reference to another text

*(unreliably) the fragments provided by other characters. Emily Brontë does much the same with the narrator/character Lockwood in 'Wuthering Heights' – a book Stevenson would surely have read. Indeed, splitting a narrative between different sources, including letters and accounts from several characters, was common in the Gothic novels of the 19th century. As Gothic novels involve strange incidents that often happen to people in isolation, there are few witnesses; each person has to tell their own story. But when another character brings those stories together, he or she does not have full knowledge of what happened. Their mistakes or uncertainty help to make the narrative harder to pin down, increasing the sense of mystery and unsettling uncertainty.*

*Utterson's perspective, which we share throughout, is unreliable. He often hears about events from other characters, interprets them wrongly, and then treats his conclusions as though they were certainties (as in the extract). Stevenson uses this as a strategy to keep wrong-footing the reader and maintain the mystery. The true situation becomes clear only in the last two chapters. Utterson never reappears after reading the documents from Lanyon and Jekyll – Stevenson has no further use for his perspective as these two narrators give their own reliable accounts and interpretations of events.*

**AO2** Identifies strategy in the structure Stevenson uses

**AO2** High-level assessment of Stevenson's technique

*Jekyll's own account can only come at the end. It fills in all the missing details that no other character could supply. Stevenson has to withhold Jekyll's perspective until the end in order to maintain the mystery. If Jekyll had told his own story earlier, we would have seen his experiments and transformations, and it would be a very different work. The various perspectives through which the story is told not only mould the structure of the novel, they are essential to its form. Stevenson fragments the narrative just as the potion fragments Jekyll, making the structure of the novel reinforce its message.*

**AO2** Relates structure to purpose

**AO1** Good summary relating back to the question and demonstrating Stevenson's use of structure

**VERY HIGH LEVEL**

**Comment:**
A clear answer which maintains discussion at a very high level. It places the evidence from the extract firmly in the context of Stevenson's approach and technique elsewhere in the text. The answer shows a sophisticated understanding of how Stevenson uses multiple perspectives, showing a confident grasp of the overall structure and form of the novel. There are some excellent points relating the text to its historical and literary context.

## Question 3

Read the following extract from *The Strange Case of Dr Jekyll and Mr Hyde* (Chapter Six, pages 32–3).

In this extract, Mr Utterson puzzles over why Dr Jekyll will not see him, and why Dr Jekyll and Dr Lanyon have fallen out.

> As soon as he got home, Utterson sat down and wrote to Jekyll, complaining of his exclusion from the house, and asking the cause of this unhappy break with Lanyon; and the next day brought him a long answer, often very pathetically worded, and sometimes
> 5   darkly mysterious in drift. The quarrel with Lanyon was incurable. 'I do not blame our old friend,' Jekyll wrote, 'but I share his view that we must never meet. I mean from henceforth to lead a life of extreme seclusion; you must not be surprised, nor must you doubt my friendship, if my door is often shut even to you. You must suffer
> 10   me to go my own dark way. I have brought on myself a punishment and a danger that I cannot name. If I am the chief of sinners, I am the chief of sufferers also. I could not think that this earth contained a place for sufferings and terrors so unmanning; and you can do but one thing, Utterson, to lighten this destiny, and that is to respect my
> 15   silence.' Utterson was amazed; the dark influence of Hyde had been withdrawn, the doctor had returned to his old tasks and amities; a week ago, the prospect had smiled with every promise of a cheerful and an honoured age; and now in a moment, friendship, and peace of mind and the whole tenor of his life were wrecked. So great and
> 20   unprepared a change pointed to madness; but in view of Lanyon's manner and words, there must lie for it some deeper ground.
>
>     A week afterwards Dr Lanyon took to his bed, and in something less than a fortnight he was dead. The night after the funeral, at which he had been sadly affected, Utterson locked the door of
> 25   his business room, and sitting there by the light of a melancholy candle, drew out and set before him an envelope addressed by the hand and sealed with the seal of his dear friend. 'PRIVATE: for the hands of J. G. Utterson ALONE and in case of his predecease to be destroyed unread', so it was emphatically superscribed; and
> 30   the lawyer dreaded to behold the contents.

Starting with this extract, explore how Stevenson creates and uses a sense of mystery.

Write about:

- how Stevenson creates and uses a sense of mystery in this extract
- how Stevenson creates and uses a sense of mystery elsewhere in the novel.

**[30 marks]**

## Annotated sample answers

Now, read the three sample answers that follow and, based on what you have read, try to allocate a level to your own work. Which of the three responses is your answer closest to? Don't be discouraged if your work doesn't seem as strong as some of the responses here – the point is to use these samples to learn about what is needed and then put it into practice in your own work. Conversely, you may have mentioned relevant ideas or points which don't appear in these responses; if this is the case, give yourself a pat on the back – it shows you are considering lots of good ideas!

### Sample answer A

**AO1** Relates the question to the whole novel

**AO3** Contextual point, but not explored

'Dr Jekyll and Mr Hyde' is a story full of mysteries. It starts with a mystery: when Utterson and Enfield come to the battered door, Enfield tells the mysterious story about Hyde crashing into a child and managing to get £100 from the person who lived behind the door, which would have been a lot of money in Victorian times. The mystery for Utterson is who Hyde is and how he got money from Jekyll, whose door it is. He says 'if he be Mr Hyde, … I shall be Mr Seek'. This is what he will do in the novel – find out answers to mysteries.

**AO1** Good use of appropriate quotation

In the extract, Utterson has been trying to solve another mystery: why Jekyll and Lanyon have fallen out and why Jekyll won't see Utterson. The letter he gets from Jekyll raises more questions rather than giving any answers. It is in very mysterious language. Jekyll must go 'his own dark way' and put up with dangers and suffering that he can't explain. He seems to be both victim and sinner or criminal. It's too hard for Utterson to work out what is going on and he thinks Jekyll might be mad. But that doesn't really answer the mystery either, as Lanyon's words and then his death suggest 'there must lie for it some deeper ground', which means there is even more mystery.

**AO2** Attempt to analyse the effects of language

**AO2** Embedded quotation supports point

**AO1** This seems to link to the first paragraph, not the second

The mysteries get even more complicated later. Why does Jekyll have such a strange will, and why won't he explain it? Why does Hyde kill Carew? Why does Jekyll run away from the window when he's talking to Enfield and Utterson? Why has Hyde apparently killed Jekyll and then himself, and where is Jekyll's body? When Lanyon sees the transformation it gets even worse. It's not possible to make a potion that changes someone, so that's another mystery. Even Jekyll doesn't answer that question, because he messed up the potion and put in chemicals with impurities so he doesn't know how it works. He also never finds out if a person can be two people at once or more than two people or something else. It's still all a mystery at the end.

**AO1** Clear grasp of different aspects of the mystery throughout the novel

**AO1** Hints at more interesting idea, but no textual evidence or development

34

**AO2** Attempt to analyse the effect of language; this new point should start in a new paragraph

**AO2** Effect identified but not analysed precisely

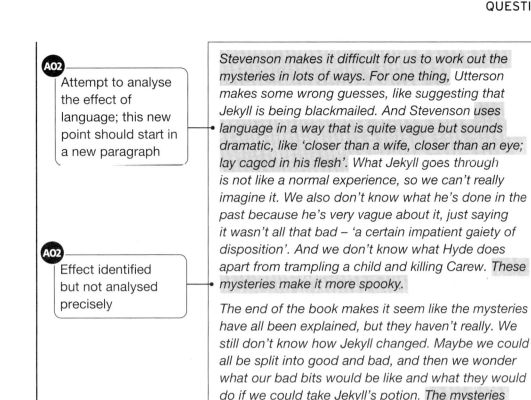

Stevenson makes it difficult for us to work out the mysteries in lots of ways. For one thing, Utterson makes some wrong guesses, like suggesting that Jekyll is being blackmailed. And Stevenson uses language in a way that is quite vague but sounds dramatic, like 'closer than a wife, closer than an eye; lay caged in his flesh'. What Jekyll goes through is not like a normal experience, so we can't really imagine it. We also don't know what he's done in the past because he's very vague about it, just saying it wasn't all that bad – 'a certain impatient gaiety of disposition'. And we don't know what Hyde does apart from trampling a child and killing Carew. These mysteries make it more spooky.

The end of the book makes it seem like the mysteries have all been explained, but they haven't really. We still don't know how Jekyll changed. Maybe we could all be split into good and bad, and then we wonder what our bad bits would be like and what they would do if we could take Jekyll's potion. The mysteries that are left over make us wonder about ourselves.

**AO1** Clear paragraph structure here: makes a point, then gives examples and evidence

**AO1** Returns to the question with a decisive conclusion

**MID LEVEL**

**Comment:**
A sound mid level answer that raises some good points. There is a lot here on how Stevenson uses mystery, but not very much detail on how he creates that sense of mystery. There is little attempt to place the novel in its literary or historical context.

**For a Good Level:**

- Pay more attention to the extract before moving on to discuss the novel as a whole.
- Make a clear examination of language and how Stevenson uses it to create effects.
- Look at the overall structure of the answer and make it flow logically, linking points together.

## Sample answer B

**AO2** — Thoughtful account of how Stevenson uses language to guide reader response

**AO1** — A key quotation stating Jekyll's view of his position, but not thoroughly explored

*There is mystery throughout the novel, and this extract gives a good example of how Stevenson builds and uses it. He helps make us see the mystery, introducing Jekyll's letter as 'darkly mysterious in drift', and ending 'Utterson was amazed', which helps to direct our own response. Stevenson spells out why Utterson is amazed: Jekyll has been freed from Hyde, his life had returned to normal – and now for no obvious reason he is despairing again. Utterson guesses Jekyll has gone mad, but even that doesn't explain it, as Lanyon's behaviour suggests 'there must lie for it some deeper ground'. This brings back the mystery. In the letter, Jekyll describes his state in a way that is quite mysterious and hard to work out: 'I am the chief of sinners, I am the chief of sufferers also'. He refers to suffering and terrors he doesn't explain, making them more scary and mysterious.*

**AO2** — Clear statement of the effects of Stevenson's choice of words

**AO3** — Attempt to link to contemporary social context, could be better expressed

*Stevenson repeats this pattern of drawing out mystery to make it more obvious. It starts with Enfield pointing out the door and saying that it is connected 'with a very odd story'. This makes us and Utterson want to hear more. The story he tells of Hyde trampling the child leads to more mysteries: who is this odd, repellent character? why does everyone hate him instinctively? how did he get the £100? The last would have been more of a mystery in the Victorian age when only smart-looking people had access to lots of money. Today, some rich people choose to look scruffy or odd, but that didn't happen in the 19th century, so Utterson assumes there is some criminal activity here. (As a lawyer, he will naturally think of crime.)*

**AO2** — Analysis of Stevenson's technique of withholding details

**AO3** — Well-chosen quotation

*The central mysteries – who or what Hyde is and how he is connected with Jekyll – build up over the course of the novel. The more Utterson tries to find out, the more mysterious it becomes. Stevenson builds the mystery by having Jekyll refuse to explain anything, but he behaves in strange ways (like hiding from Enfield and Utterson at the window). Also, he shows us very little of Hyde. Utterson's thoughts after meeting Hyde concentrate on what he can't pin down – the mysterious: 'There is something more, if I could find a name for it.'*

**AO3** — Places the novel in its literary context

*Stevenson also uses the setting and atmosphere to add to the mystery. When Utterson goes with Inspector Newcomen to visit Hyde's lodgings, they drive through a strange landscape, half-hidden by fog so that it seems like 'some city in a nightmare'. Things half-seen add to the mystery, in a way common in Gothic novels which frequently use darkness, fog, strange mental states and other ways of stopping characters seeing clearly. The maid faints part-way through watching the attack on Carew, and Poole only glimpses a figure hiding among the crates.*

*In the final chapter, Jekyll explains lots of the mysteries behind the events of the novel, but creates some new mysteries. The death of Jekyll/ Hyde leaves many questions unanswered. Although Jekyll says that 'others will outstrip me on the same lines', it's hard to see which mysteries other people will solve. Questions about what makes up a human and the role of evil are left just hinted at. It doesn't seem likely science can solve them, even Jekyll's 'transcendental' sort of science.*

**AO1**

Introduces but does not explore a further dimension of mystery in the novel

**GOOD LEVEL**

**Comment:**

A thoughtful, considered response, with some close attention to how Stevenson uses language to build mystery. There is a good command of the novel as a whole, and appropriate choice and embedding of relevant quotations. The final paragraph raises issues that could have been explored further. There is some attempt to place the novel in context – more successfully regarding the Gothic than in relation to Hyde's appearance.

**For a High Level:**

- Comment on the structure of the novel and how Stevenson uses this to serve the mystery.
- Extend the discussion of mysteries beyond the plot-driven puzzles to explore ideas raised briefly in the final paragraph.
- Refer to the emerging genre of detective fiction as a model for posing and solving mystery through plot.

## Sample answer C

 **A01**

Introduction skilfully relates question to macro and micro structure of the novel

'Jekyll and Hyde' has mystery at its heart, and although partly resolved, plenty remains unexplained. It is also built up from smaller mysteries, so that the closer we look the more tiny mysteries we find.

The extract shows how Stevenson uses mystery to build his plot and to create the tone and atmosphere in the novel. Jekyll's response to Utterson's letter only repeats Utterson's points more forcefully without answering them. It hints at more dire circumstances than Utterson fears. He intensifies the mystery by saying that he 'cannot name' the dangers, and by using cryptic phrasing: he faces both 'punishments and dangers', he is 'the chief of sinners' and 'the chief of sufferers also', and must go his 'own dark way'. After reading the letter, 'Utterson was amazed', and Stevenson puts his reaction in a form which further suggests mystery: Jekyll's life had improved, so why this change for the worse?

**A02**

Excellent choice of quotations, successfully embedded to show how Stevenson uses language

Just as this episode is constructed around mystery, so is the entire plot. At the centre is the mystery of who Hyde is and what his relationship is with Jekyll. Smaller mysteries play around this – why does Jekyll's will mention his 'death or disappearance'? What makes Hyde so repellent? Why does he seem to have no history, so that the police can learn nothing about him? The plot thickens, with mysteries piled on one another, some of them red herrings: why does Jekyll apparently forge a letter from Hyde? Why does he seek a particular chemical? Why does he rush from the window when speaking to Utterson and Enfield? Although the crime and mystery novels we know now did not exist in the same form, Stevenson seems to be inching towards them in the novel, with the central question not a 'whodunit?' but a 'who is it?'.

**A02**

Relates the question to the structure of the novel

**A03**

Relates novel to literary context

**A01**

Reinforces link to the question when introducing a new topic

In the extract and elsewhere, Stevenson also creates and uses mystery to intensify horror. Jekyll's extravagant and ambiguous language creates a sense of the horror he is experiencing: 'I could not think that this earth contained a place for sufferings and terrors so unmanning'. This is characteristic of Gothic novels, one of the genres on which Stevenson draws to construct the novel. It is a powerful technique as it leaves us free to imagine whatever we would find most horrific: the unknown or unnamed is always more potent than anything specific.

**A02**

Detailed analysis of language used to create an effect

**A03**

Appropriate link to literary context

**A02**

Convincing analysis of how effects work

Stevenson uses this technique repeatedly. He leaves most of Hyde's crimes mysterious, so that we imagine whatever we each feel is most terrible. We *do not even know the nature of the 'irregularities' Jekyll was committing when he set about his research, which is unsettling – how bad were they really? We don't know enough about Jekyll's own sense of morality to be able to tell.*

*Even when we know from Lanyon's letter that Jekyll transforms into Hyde, much mystery remains. Jekyll's statement uses extravagant imagery again, talking about the 'dreadful shipwreck' of his condition and the struggle in his 'agonized womb of consciousness'. Our sense of what Jekyll feels lies in the gap between his experience (which is so alien we can't imagine it) and the imagery.*

**AO2** Precise insight into how an effect is created through the limitations of expression

*Even when Jekyll reveals what has happened, mysteries about details remain (including what is in the potion), and larger philosophical mysteries are raised: how are good and evil linked in a person? what is evil and its source? is evil natural? Jekyll's 'partial discovery' has had terrible consequences, suggesting an even greater mystery: are there things that cannot or should not be known? This was an important question in the 19th century, as new discoveries in science were showing that some knowledge taken for granted was wrong, and were challenging religious beliefs and traditions. Some people argued against exploring everything with science and trying to explain everything, removing its mystery. Stevenson's novel reflects this fear of science.*

**AO1** Introduces the larger issues raised by the novel

**AO3** Convincing exploration of intellectual context

## VERY HIGH LEVEL

**Comment:**

An answer at a very high level that expands skilfully from the extract to the novel as a whole. The answer engages fully with the question and shows in detail how a sense of mystery is created through Stevenson's use of language, as well as demonstrating how he uses mystery. Considerable insight is demonstrated, and the answer is convincingly argued. The novel is clearly placed in its historical, literary and intellectual context.

## Question 4

Read the following extract from *The Strange Case of Dr Jekyll and Mr Hyde* (Chapter Ten, pages 59–60).

In this extract, Dr Jekyll describes his first experience of taking the potion.

> Enough, then, that I not only recognized my natural body for the mere aura and effulgence of certain of the powers that made up my spirit, but managed to compound a drug by which these powers should be dethroned from their supremacy, and a
> 5   second form and countenance substituted, none the less natural to me because they were the expression, and bore the stamp, of lower elements in my soul.
>
> I hesitated long before I put this theory to the test of practice. I knew well that I risked death; for any drug that so potently
> 10   controlled and shook the very fortress of identity, might by the least scruple of an overdose or at the least inopportunity in the moment of exhibition, utterly blot out that immaterial tabernacle which I looked to it to change. But the temptation of a discovery so singular and profound, at last overcame the suggestions of
> 15   alarm. I had long since prepared my tincture; I purchased at once, from a firm of wholesale chemists, a large quantity of a particular salt which I knew, from my experiments, to be the last ingredient required; and late one accursed night, I compounded the elements, watched them boil and smoke together in the
> 20   glass, and when the ebullition had subsided, with a strong glow of courage, drank off the potion.
>
> The most racking pangs succeeded: a grinding in the bones, deadly nausea, and a horror of the spirit that cannot be exceeded at the hour of birth or death. Then these agonies
> 25   began swiftly to subside, and I came to myself as if out of a great sickness. There was something strange in my sensations, something indescribably new and, from its very novelty, incredibly sweet.

Starting with this extract, explore how Stevenson presents attitudes to science in the novel.

Write about:

- how Stevenson presents attitudes to science in this extract
- how Stevenson presents attitudes to science in the novel as a whole.

**[30 marks]**

## Annotated sample answers

Now, read the three sample answers that follow and, based on what you have read, try to allocate a level to your own work. Which of the three responses is your answer closest to? Don't be discouraged if your work doesn't seem as strong as some of the responses here – the point is to use these samples to learn about what is needed and then put it into practice in your own work. Conversely, you may have mentioned relevant ideas or points which don't appear in these responses; if this is the case, give yourself a pat on the back – it shows you are considering lots of good ideas!

## Sample answer A

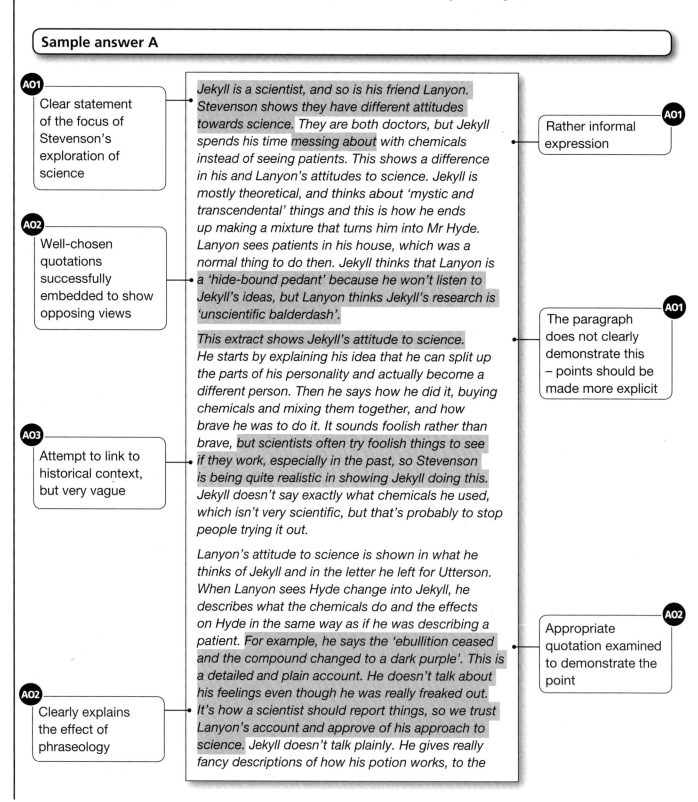

**AO1** — Clear statement of the focus of Stevenson's exploration of science

*Jekyll is a scientist, and so is his friend Lanyon. Stevenson shows they have different attitudes towards science. They are both doctors, but Jekyll spends his time messing about with chemicals instead of seeing patients. This shows a difference in his and Lanyon's attitudes to science. Jekyll is mostly theoretical, and thinks about 'mystic and transcendental' things and this is how he ends up making a mixture that turns him into Mr Hyde. Lanyon sees patients in his house, which was a normal thing to do then. Jekyll thinks that Lanyon is a 'hide-bound pedant' because he won't listen to Jekyll's ideas, but Lanyon thinks Jekyll's research is 'unscientific balderdash'.*

**AO1** — Rather informal expression

**AO2** — Well-chosen quotations successfully embedded to show opposing views

*This extract shows Jekyll's attitude to science. He starts by explaining his idea that he can split up the parts of his personality and actually become a different person. Then he says how he did it, buying chemicals and mixing them together, and how brave he was to do it. It sounds foolish rather than brave, but scientists often try foolish things to see if they work, especially in the past, so Stevenson is being quite realistic in showing Jekyll doing this. Jekyll doesn't say exactly what chemicals he used, which isn't very scientific, but that's probably to stop people trying it out.*

**AO1** — The paragraph does not clearly demonstrate this – points should be made more explicit

**AO3** — Attempt to link to historical context, but very vague

*Lanyon's attitude to science is shown in what he thinks of Jekyll and in the letter he left for Utterson. When Lanyon sees Hyde change into Jekyll, he describes what the chemicals do and the effects on Hyde in the same way as if he was describing a patient. For example, he says the 'ebullition ceased and the compound changed to a dark purple'. This is a detailed and plain account. He doesn't talk about his feelings even though he was really freaked out. It's how a scientist should report things, so we trust Lanyon's account and approve of his approach to science. Jekyll doesn't talk plainly. He gives really fancy descriptions of how his potion works, to the*

**AO2** — Appropriate quotation examined to demonstrate the point

**AO2** — Clearly explains the effect of phraseology

**A01**

Personal point would be better made in more general and objective terms

**A03**

Places the work in its historical context, but no firm conclusion drawn

*point where it's sometimes hard to understand what he means. For example, when he's scared the potion will kill him, he says it might 'utterly blot out that immaterial tabernacle'. This is not good science writing. Lanyon is more like a real scientist. Jekyll seems like someone who would think homeopathy and crystal-healing work, and try to persuade people it's scientific. But, like Lanyon, we are in for a shock when it turns out Jekyll's potion really does work.*

*Stevenson cleverly sets up one scientist who takes a real scientific approach and one who's got side-tracked into spiritual things and then shows the second one being right, which is a surprise. In the late 19th century, lots of people believed in things like spiritualism and even Conan Doyle, the author of 'Sherlock Holmes', thought fairies were real. Some people thought science was distracting people from God and their spiritual side, so Stevenson might be saying something about that but it's hard to tell what he really thought. He makes Jekyll use science to do something Lanyon thinks is impossible. The result is Lanyon dies because he can't face being wrong, or science being different than he thought it was. But Jekyll dies as well, so we don't know for certain what Stevenson thought.*

**A02**

Effective selection of a quotation to show Stevenson making a point through language; could be phrased more formally

**A01**

Concise summary of Stevenson's technique

**MID LEVEL**

**Comment:**

Shows knowledge of the text and how science is presented, including the clear difference between Jekyll and Lanyon's attitudes. There is some attempt to place the discussion in the wider historical context and to relate the novel to Stevenson's engagement with contemporary debate. Some of the phraseology is rather informal, and the answer favours a modern view of science, which sometimes colours the discussion unhelpfully.

**For a Good Level:**

- Make a clearer connection with the question and indicate the direction of the essay in the opening paragraph.
- Use more quotation from the text, properly embedded, to show in detail how Stevenson creates an effect.
- Give the essay a clearer structure, with links between points, and clearly widen the discussion from the extract to the rest of the novel.
- Try to give a more balanced view, and explore the tension rather than taking sides.

## Sample answer B

The novel is about a scientist, Henry Jekyll, and his dangerous experiment to split his psyche, producing his alter ego, Mr Hyde. As such, science plays an important part in the story.

In this extract, we see a bit of Jekyll's own attitude towards science. He sees it as a way of trying out his ideas about the human personality. Like many other scientists, he tries his experiment on himself. He knows it's dangerous, but acts properly like a scientist in thinking through his test and recording carefully what happens when he takes the potion. His account of the 'racking pangs', 'grinding in the bones' and 'deadly nausea' is the sort of description a doctor would give of a patient, or a patient might give to a doctor. But then he uses more exotic language (which is more characteristic of him), as he describes a 'horror of the spirit that cannot be exceeded at the hour of birth or death'. This is something science doesn't have language for.

While Jekyll sees science as a tool he can use in exploring his philosophical ideas, his friend Dr Lanyon has a different approach. Stevenson uses him to contrast with Jekyll. Lanyon thinks Jekyll's attitude is 'too fanciful' and his ideas are 'balderdash'. He is a practical, down-to-earth scientist. When he sees the transformation of Hyde, he tries to describe it carefully, saying how Hyde 'reeled, staggered, clutched at the table', and how 'his face became suddenly black and the features seemed to melt and alter'. But he can't stay calm. He hides his face behind his arm, his 'mind submerged in terror'. By doing this, Stevenson shows the limitations of Lanyon's attitude towards science – he literally can't face what is in front of him. Although Lanyon ridicules Jekyll's attitude, it seems in the end Jekyll was right and science is more than the 'narrow and material' thing that Lanyon thinks it is.

It's ironic that Jekyll hesitates for a long time before taking his potion, worried that the 'the least inopportunity in the moment of exhibition' might be fatal. In fact, the potion only works because his chemicals are not pure enough. Stevenson's science doesn't stand up to close examination. If Jekyll had worked out how to make this potion (which already seems pretty unlikely) it shouldn't work if one ingredient is impure unless his recipe was wrong. Then he'd be pretty lucky if the impurity made it work rather than, say, killed him. This suggests that Stevenson is not really interested in whether the science is realistic, he just wants to make a point with it. It's a bit like in Mary Shelley's 'Frankenstein'

**A01** The question asks about 'attitudes to science', not just 'science'

**A02** Examines Stevenson's use of language using appropriate quotations

**A01** Picks up on idea, but could make more of this point

**A02** Clear statement of Stevenson's technique, linking back to the question

**A02** Quotations successfully embedded and used to support a point

**A02** Good analysis of Stevenson's technique

**A01** Need a link to move on to this point, which does not follow logically from the last

**A01** Attempt at personal interpretation supported by evidence

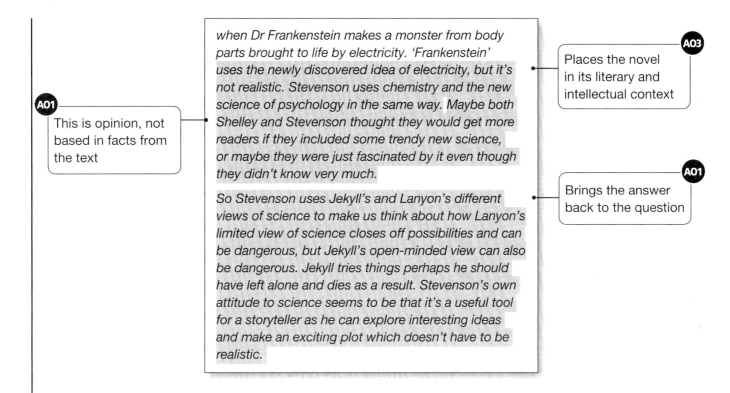

**AO1**

This is opinion, not based in facts from the text

when Dr Frankenstein makes a monster from body parts brought to life by electricity. 'Frankenstein' uses the newly discovered idea of electricity, but it's not realistic. Stevenson uses chemistry and the new science of psychology in the same way. Maybe both Shelley and Stevenson thought they would get more readers if they included some trendy new science, or maybe they were just fascinated by it even though they didn't know very much.

So Stevenson uses Jekyll's and Lanyon's different views of science to make us think about how Lanyon's limited view of science closes off possibilities and can be dangerous, but Jekyll's open-minded view can also be dangerous. Jekyll tries things perhaps he should have left alone and dies as a result. Stevenson's own attitude to science seems to be that it's a useful tool for a storyteller as he can explore interesting ideas and make an exciting plot which doesn't have to be realistic.

**AO3**

Places the novel in its literary and intellectual context

**AO1**

Brings the answer back to the question

**GOOD LEVEL**

**Comment:**

Some good ideas introduced and supported by appropriate quotations that are successfully embedded in the argument. There is some relation of the novel to its contemporary context, and an appropriate link with another text (*Frankenstein*). It sometimes strays too far from the question and needs bringing back; the opening suggests a misreading of the question as being about science itself rather than attitudes to science.

**For a High Level:**

■ Stick more closely to the question and make sure that all points relate to it.

■ Explore in more detail what the issues are that Stevenson is examining through the attitudes towards science shown in the novel.

■ Discuss Jekyll's aims and interests explicitly, and why Lanyon considers them unscientific. Does Stevenson endorse either view?

## Sample answer C

**AO1** Sets framework for the discussion

*Science is a central theme in 'Dr Jekyll and Mr Hyde'. Stevenson approaches it through the differing attitudes towards science of Dr Jekyll and Dr Lanyon. Both are experienced scientists, probably of about the same standing, so the contrast and argument between them is a good space for Stevenson to explore ideas.*

**AO1** Considered approach to the question, placing it in the context of the whole novel

*In this extract, we see something of Jekyll's attitude to science. It is quite a difficult passage because it explains Jekyll's unusual theories about the nature of human beings and his scientific thinking. He first explains that he believes that the spiritual character of a person's 'natural' body affects their appearance, so his normal form is the 'effulgence of certain of the powers that made up my spirit'. His scientific discovery was a way of letting a different part of his personality produce his physical appearance. Hyde expresses the 'lower elements' of his soul. This reflects the contemporary interest in physiognomy, which claimed to find clues to a person's character in their physical appearance. In the second paragraph he describes what he did. In this way, Stevenson grounds Jekyll's strange theories in the more familiar image of science as chemicals, potions, and the physical effects of medicines or poisons.*

**AO2** Shows detailed understanding of difficult passage

**AO3** Places the novel in its historical context

**AO2** Explores effects of placement of material in the text

**AO1** Convincing statement of contrasting attitudes

*Jekyll explains his own approach to science as leaning towards 'the mystic and transcendental'. This contrasts with the very practical, objective approach of Lanyon, and makes it easy for Lanyon to criticise Jekyll's work as 'too fanciful' and 'unscientific balderdash'. Stevenson uses the contrast between the two characters to show very different attitudes towards science. Lanyon's own approach is shown in his account of Hyde's transformation into Jekyll. He gives a detailed description of the mixing of the chemicals, the bubbling and colour change, and a clinical description of Hyde and the effects of the potion.*

**AO1** Links discussion back to the question

**AO1** Insightful personal response

*Jekyll considers Lanyon 'an ignorant, blatant pedant'. Lanyon embodies the limitations of the scientist so 'hidebound' by current theories that his 'narrow and material' worldview can't cope with something new. This is the opposite of how science should be: any theory can be overturned by new evidence. While Jekyll was only suggesting his ideas, Lanyon had good reason to be sceptical, but after witnessing the transformation he remains 'incredulous'. 'My life is shaken to its roots,' he says – he can't believe or process what he has seen.*

*The 19th century saw great progress in chemistry and medicine. Stevenson places Jekyll at the*

forefront of experimentation but we don't know what to make of him. He could be mad or deluded, as Lanyon originally thinks, or he could be on the brink of great discoveries, as Jekyll thinks himself. Many great scientists have been ridiculed or criticised for revolutionary ideas, and Jekyll sees himself in this mould, fighting against Lanyon's view of his 'scientific heresies'. One area of scientific progress at the time 'Dr Jekyll and Mr Hyde' was written was psychology. The idea of approaching the human spirit through science was therefore a current concern. Some people ridiculed or dismissed it, some were excited by it and some thought it was dangerous or even blasphemous. Stevenson explores this contemporary concern in his novel.

Science lies at the heart of 'Dr Jekyll and Mr Hyde', since the mystery of the plot hinges on Jekyll's scientific experiments. Science is also the root of the discord between Jekyll and Lanyon. The attitudes shown by Jekyll and Lanyon reflect those found in Victorian society, and in exploring them in his novel Stevenson approaches a fundamental question that is still relevant today: are there places science should not go? Are there things best left undiscovered? Jekyll found to his cost that once he had unleashed Hyde, he couldn't lock him away again. Is the human urge to keep exploring as far as possible something that can't be stopped? The novel ends with Jekyll's statement, so he has the last word. He assumes others will 'outstrip' him, so this dangerous experiment will go on. Yet it has brought him to his death; it is a poor outlook for the people who follow in his footsteps.

**A03** Thoroughly relates the theme to its historical context

**A03** Relates the novel to its intellectual context

**A01** Skilful introduction of personal response

**A01** Precise analysis of what Stevenson achieves by using attitudes to science

**VERY HIGH LEVEL**

**Comment:**
The answer maintains a high level of discussion, consistently referring back to the question and presenting a sound critical argument. It moves skilfully from the detail of how Stevenson communicates attitudes to the broader picture, assessing with insight what he achieves by exploring them. The answer convincingly locates the issue in the context of science and attitudes towards science in the 19th century.

# PART THREE: FURTHER YORK NOTES PRACTICE TESTS WITH SHORT ANSWERS

Here are three further questions on the text in a similar style to the ones you might face in your exam. Taking into account what you have learnt from the mark schemes on pages 7–8, and the sample responses to the other questions, use Questions 5 to 7 as you wish. You may choose to:

■ plan ideas

■ write opening paragraphs or part answers

■ write full answers at your own speed

■ write full answers to a set time limit.

Once you have finished, you can check to see if you have covered some of the key points suggested in the Answers section, and make a judgement about what level you have achieved.

## Question 5

Read the following extract from *The Strange Case of Dr Jekyll and Mr Hyde* (Chapter Ten, pages 67–8).

In this extract, Dr Jekyll describes Hyde's attack on Sir Danvers Carew and its aftermath.

> Instantly the spirit of hell awoke in me and raged. With a
> transport of glee, I mauled the unresisting body, tasting delight
> from every blow; and it was not till weariness had begun to
> succeed, that I was suddenly, in the top fit of my delirium, struck
> 5   through the heart by a cold thrill of terror. A mist dispersed;
> I saw my life to be forfeit; and fled from the scene of these
> excesses, at once glorying and trembling, my lust of evil gratified
> and stimulated, my love of life screwed to the topmost peg.
> I ran to the house in Soho, and (to make assurance doubly
> 10   sure) destroyed my papers; thence I set out through the lamplit
> streets, in the same divided ecstasy of mind, gloating on my
> crime, light-headedly devising others in the future, and yet still
> hastening and still hearkening in my wake for the steps of the
> avenger. Hyde had a song upon his lips as he compounded the
> 15   draught, and as he drank it, pledged the dead man. The pangs
> of transformation had not done tearing him, before Henry Jekyll,
> with streaming tears of gratitude and remorse, had fallen upon
> his knees and lifted his clasped hands to God. The veil of self-
> indulgence was rent from head to foot, I saw my life as a whole:
> 20   I followed it up from the days of childhood, when I had walked
> with my father's hand, and through the self-denying toils of my
> professional life, to arrive again and again, with the same sense
> of unreality, at the damned horrors of the evening. I could have
> screamed aloud; I sought with tears and prayers to smother
> 25   down the crowd of hideous images and sounds with which my
> memory swarmed against me; and still, between the petitions,
> the ugly face of my iniquity stared into my soul. As the acuteness
> of this remorse began to die away, it was succeeded by a
> sense of joy. The problem of my conduct was solved. Hyde was
> 30   thenceforth impossible …

'Stevenson uses extravagant language in place of plot.'

Starting with this extract, explore how far you agree with this opinion.

Write about:

■ how Stevenson uses extravagant language in this extract

■ how Stevenson uses extravagant language elsewhere in the novel.

**[30 marks]**

## Question 6

Read the following extract from *The Strange Case of Dr Jekyll and Mr Hyde* (Chapter Four, pages 22–3).

In this extract, Mr Utterson drives through London with Inspector Newcomen to Hyde's apartment.

> It was by this time about nine in the morning, and the first fog of the season. A great chocolate-coloured pall lowered over heaven, but the wind was continually charging and routing these embattled vapours; so that as the cab crawled from street
> 5 to street, Mr Utterson beheld a marvellous number of degrees and hues of twilight; for here it would be dark like the back-end of evening; and there would be a glow of a rich, lurid brown, like the light of some strange conflagration; and here, for a moment, the fog would be quite broken up, and a haggard shaft
> 10 of daylight would glance in between the swirling wreaths. The dismal quarter of Soho seen under these changing glimpses, with its muddy ways, and slatternly passengers, and its lamps, which had never been extinguished or had been kindled afresh to combat this mournful reinvasion of darkness, seemed, in
> 15 the lawyer's eyes, like a district of some city in a nightmare. The thoughts of his mind, besides, were of the gloomiest dye; and when he glanced at the companion of his drive, he was conscious of some touch of that terror of the law and the law's officers, which may at times assail the most honest.
>
> 20 As the cab drew up before the address indicated, the fog lifted a little and showed him a dingy street, a gin palace, a low French eating house, a shop for the retail of penny numbers and twopenny salads, many ragged children huddled in the doorways, and many women of many different nationalities
> 25 passing out, key in hand, to have a morning glass; and the next moment the fog settled down again upon that part, as brown as umber, and cut him off from his blackguardly surroundings.

Starting with this extract, explore how Stevenson creates a threatening atmosphere.

Write about:

- how Stevenson creates a threatening atmosphere in this extract
- how Stevenson creates a threatening atmosphere elsewhere in the novel.

**[30 marks]**

## Question 7

Read the following extract from *The Strange Case of Dr Jekyll and Mr Hyde* (Chapter Eight, pages 39–40).

In this extract, Poole explains to Mr Utterson the changes that have come over Dr Jekyll that have aroused his suspicions.

'All this last week (you must know) him, or it, or whatever it is that lives in that cabinet, has been crying night and day for some sort of medicine and cannot get it to his mind. It was sometimes his way – the master's, that is – to write his orders on a sheet of
5 paper and throw it on the stair. We've had nothing else this week back; nothing but papers, and a closed door, and the very meals left there to be smuggled in when nobody was looking. Well, sir, every day, ay, and twice and thrice in the same day, there have been orders and complaints, and I have been sent flying to all the
10 wholesale chemists in town. Every time I brought the stuff back, there would be another paper telling me to return it, because it was not pure, and another order to a different firm. This drug is wanted bitter bad, sir, whatever for.'

'Have you any of these papers?' asked Mr Utterson.

15 Poole felt in his pocket and handed out a crumpled note, which the lawyer, bending nearer to the candle, carefully examined. Its contents ran thus: 'Dr Jekyll presents his compliments to Messrs Maw. He assures them that their last sample is impure and quite useless for his present purpose. In
20 the year 18—, Dr J. purchased a somewhat large quantity from Messrs M. He now begs them to search with most sedulous care, and should any of the same quality be left, to forward it to him at once. Expense is no consideration. The importance of this to Dr J. can hardly be exaggerated.' So far the letter had run
25 composedly enough, but here with a sudden splutter of the pen, the writer's emotion had broken loose. 'For God's sake,' he had added, 'find me some of the old.'

'This is a strange note,' said Mr Utterson; and then sharply, 'How do you come to have it open?'

30 'The man at Maw's was main angry, sir, and he threw it back to me like so much dirt,' returned Poole.

Starting with this extract, explore how Stevenson uses Poole and other minor characters in the novel.

Write about:

■ how Stevenson uses Poole in this extract

■ how Stevenson uses Poole and other minor characters elsewhere in the novel.

**[30 marks]**

# ANSWERS

Short (indicative content) answers are given for Questions 5 to 7 below and on the following pages, covering the three main Assessment Objectives.

## Question 5

**Your answer could include the following:**

### AO1

- Extravagant language is used to express heightened emotions throughout the novel, e.g. in the extract: 'the spirit of hell awoke in me and raged.' Explain when and by whom it is used elsewhere in the novel.

- Extravagant language is also used to shape our response to events, e.g. in Chapter Four, Utterson rides with Inspector Newcomen to Hyde's lodgings; he describes the area, and says that it seemed 'like a district of some city in a nightmare'. By giving Utterson's response, Stevenson encourages us to see the scene as sinister and frightening.

- Instead of describing events, Stevenson describes their effects on people, using extravagant language, e.g. in the extract, 'tasting delight from every blow'.

- Events are often described vaguely but using emotive or arresting terms, e.g. in the extract, 'mauled the unresisting body'.

### AO2

- Evocative words words are chosen to describe extreme actions or sensations (and their effects) in the extract, e.g. 'roaring', 'blasted', 'plunged', 'curse', 'shipwreck', 'agonies'.

- Emotionally laden terms are piled up, e.g. 'a dismal screech of mere animal terror', 'abnormal and misbegotten'.

- Language is used to produce an emotional response in the reader; explain how it works, e.g. in Chapter Eight, Poole reports that Hyde/Jekyll cried out 'like a rat'. Most people find rats repellent, so this makes us recoil (as Poole did).

- Vivid and unusual imagery is used, including metaphor and simile, e.g. in the extract, 'The veil of self-indulgence was rent from head to foot'.

- Unusual or obscure words force readers to focus and concentrate, e.g. in the extract, 'the amorphous dust gesticulated and sinned'.

### AO3

- Extravagant language portraying extreme emotion and exotic imagery is a feature of Gothic literature.

- The detailed language of science reflects the interest in new scientific developments, often considered exotic or dangerous in the 19th century.

- While much Gothic literature has lots of incidents, making a very dense plot (and often long novels), Stevenson includes relatively few incidents but focuses on making them vivid.

## Question 6

**Your answer could include the following:**

### AO1

- Scenes or events are half-seen or glimpsed; in the extract, the swirling fog and poor light hides the view outside the cab window. Elsewhere in the novel, Poole glimpses Hyde scurrying among the crates in the shadows.

- Mystery is often associated with the sinister and unpleasant character of Hyde; a sense of threat comes from the feeling that he is evil or cruel. For example, in Chapter Two, Hyde hisses and 'snarled aloud into a savage laugh' when questioned by Utterson.

- We don't know Hyde's motives for violence so there is nothing predictable, creating a sense of unease and danger.

- There is no reliable source of information in the novel – Utterson doesn't know what is happening, and Jekyll (and Lanyon) refuse to give information.

- The familiar is contrasted with the out of the ordinary, e.g. the apparently normal, cosy scene in Jekyll's cabinet on the last night, disrupted by the twitching body of Hyde.

- We share the terror of characters in the novel; their fear is contagious and creates an air of menace.

### AO2

- Utterson feels threatened and that extends to us: in the extract, he is 'conscious of some touch of that terror of the law and the law's officers'.

- In the extract, the convoluted structure of sentences (except the first) mimics the thought processes of Utterson's troubled mind; the difficulty of following the sentences makes us feel insecure and anxious.

- The slow build-up to events creates a sense of menace, piling up details of mystery, misery, fear and anxiety. In the extract, the drawn-out description of the journey builds tension and threat before the arrival at Hyde's lodgings.

- Setting is used to create a sense of threat in the extract and elsewhere, e.g. as Utterson waits to intercept Hyde in Chapter Two.

- In the extract, words reminiscent of struggle and death – 'routing', 'embattled', 'wreaths' – create a sense of threat. Unsettling imagery is common elsewhere in the novel, e.g. 'caged in his flesh' and 'the animal within me licking the chops of memory'.

### AO3

- In the extract, the dark, foggy scene in London reflects the thick, poisonous fogs that plagued London in the 19th and early 20th centuries – the image would have carried extra threat for Stevenson's original audience, aware of the fog's dangers.

- The London streets were the scene of violent crime, which makes the trampling of the child and the murder of Carew seem likely to a contemporary audience.

- Progress in science made many people uneasy in the 19th century; Stevenson taps into this with his account of a strange, colour-changing potion that has devastating effects on Jekyll.

- References to other literature or traditions are frequently to sinister or unnatural events or beings, such as the finger writing on the wall at Nebuchadnezzar's feast.

## Question 7

**Your answer could include the following:**

### AO1

- In this extract, Poole fills in details of Jekyll's recent behaviour that Utterson could not know.

- Poole's language in the extract suggests an interpretation of Jekyll's behaviour.

- Elsewhere in the novel, other minor characters provide reports of events Utterson has not witnessed, including Enfield, the maid and Inspector Newcomen.

- In Chapter Five, the clerk, Mr Guest, provides information in the form of expertise Utterson doesn't have, examining the handwriting of the letter supposedly from Hyde.

- In Chapter Four, Hyde's landlady both gives information and shows by her attitude that Hyde is not popular.

### AO2

- Stevenson uses minor characters to give more direct, blunt accounts than the more 'cultured' characters give, e.g. in the extract, 'there have been orders and complaints, and I have been sent flying'.

- Minor characters give not only an account of events but their interpretation of them, e.g. in the extract, 'This drug is wanted bitter bad'.

- Minor characters are given little distinctive development as individual personalities, but are defined by their social status and their role in the narrative.

- The working-class minor characters share a very similar voice, which comes across in the way they speak, e.g. 'The man at Maw's was main angry, sir, and he threw it back to me like so much dirt'.

- Minor characters provide stylistic contrast with the major characters, who are their social superiors, adding variety to the writing.

### AO3

- The treatment and behaviour of working-class minor characters reflects Victorian attitudes towards class and the treatment of poorer people.

- Stevenson gives all the minor characters the same 'working-class' voice, with irregular grammar and simple vocabulary, reflecting the contemporary perception of working-class people.

- The attack on Sir Danvers Carew relies for some of its impact on the way a Victorian audience would have viewed an assault on a character with his social and professional status.